31 Verses and Prayers for the ANXIOUS MIND AND HEART

A Hope-filled and Healing Devotional for Those with Anxiety and/or Depression

By: Ashley Willis

This book is dedicated to my husband, Dave.

Sweetie, I am forever grateful that you stood by my side, prayed for me, and encouraged me to get the help that I so desperately needed during one of the darkest seasons of my life. I wouldn't be able to write this book or have the courage to talk about my own struggle with anxiety and depression without your constant love and support.

Thank you for loving me the way that you do.
I love you.

Letter to the Reader

Dear Reader,

Whether you purchased this devotional for yourself or received it as a gift, I truly believe that it is no accident that you are reading this right now. I believe that God has lead you to this book for a very specific reason—He wants you to find healing from your anxiety and depression. He wants you to walk in freedom—to live life to the fullest. He wants you to know how deeply He loves you and that He is walking through this with you. You are not alone, sweet friend. You *will* get through this. Healing begins today.

Your Sister in Christ,
Ashley

The Quiet Struggle

According to the Anxiety and Depression Association of America, "Anxiety disorders are the most common mental illness in the U.S., affecting **40 million adults** in the United States age 18 and older…, as researched by the National Institute of Mental Health." The organization also said, "Anxiety disorders are highly treatable, yet **only about one-third** of those suffering **receive treatment**."

And, when left untreated, it can take a tremendous toll on one's marriage and family.

About twelve years ago, I started experiencing depression and anxiety firsthand. But, I didn't realize it at the time. That's the funny thing about these disorders. We think its normal at first, so we struggle quietly.

Human beings are prone to having some anxious thoughts. We tell ourselves things like, "I'm just *worried*. I'll snap out of it in time."
Or,
"I'm just *down*. I'll get better when my circumstances get better."
Or,
"I'm just *a little nervous*. It will pass."

All people have these thoughts a time or two, but those suffering with anxiety and depression let these "every now and then" thoughts turn into HABITUAL AND ACCUSING thoughts. They fester and become more sinister by the day.

We suffer in silence and shame.

Over time, those of us with anxiety and depression start thinking and BELIEVING thoughts like, **"I will NEVER snap out of this. I must have done something terribly wrong to feel this way." Or, "I'm going to *lose* everything and completely *mess up* my family." Or, "If anyone knew the worries and horrible thoughts that I have, they would hate me. I can't tell anyone about this."**

Friend, if any of these sound familiar, then you know the pain of living with anxiety and depression. And, you have what I call "functional" anxiety and depression if you live with the weight of this every single day, but you are still able to complete your basic responsibilities as a spouse, a parent, a worker, etc. **However, your heart aches every day as you are riddled with accusing thoughts, a churning stomach, and heavy breathing.**

You may even experience intense anxiety attacks too. You feel like you can't tell anyone because you don't understand what brought this on, and you don't expect anyone else to either.

Friend, I'm here to tell you that **YOU ARE NOT ALONE**.

And, **YOU DID NOT DO ANYTHING TO BRING THIS ON**.

And, most importantly, **YOU CAN GET THE HELP THAT YOU NEED.**

In fact, **YOU MUST**.

I tell you this as someone who walked through a long battle with anxiety and depression.

I know how hard it is on a marriage and kids. I understand how it feels to wake up in the middle of the night in a cold sweat, having a full-blown anxiety attack, and running to the bathroom to throw up. I know the overwhelming fears of losing your spouse and the frustration of not being able to just "snap out of it."

It's gut-wrenching and heart-breaking, but **THERE IS HOPE.**

There is hope when we open up to our spouse and family about our struggle. We cannot keep it in. The only way we can get help is by being honest and open.

Hope is not hiding in the dark; it can *only* be found in the light.

So, we must be brave and bring our truth to light through sharing our deepest fears, worries, and anxieties with those we love most.

In my own experience, I wouldn't have survived my four year battle with anxiety and depression without the full support of my husband, Dave. There were times I would wake him up in the middle of the night to ask for **prayer and an encouraging word**. He lovingly prayed for me and encouraged me every single time. I truly believe that God heard our prayers and strengthened both of us through that difficult time. **Prayer has been and continues to be my life line of hope.**

Dave also encouraged me to go to **Christian counseling**. This was a tremendous help. I attended counseling on a weekly basis. Each session, my counselors would help me to unpack the root of my depression and anxiety, give me practical tools to help with my healing, and remind of the truth of God's Word.

I felt lighter and lighter with every appointment.

Today, I am living in freedom, and I am quick to tell anyone suffering with depression and anxiety that YOU CAN LIVE IN FREEDOM TOO.

Your battle with anxiety and depression doesn't define your life, so please don't let it.

Every battle requires a fight, so we must keep on fighting against the anxiety and depression by resisting the desire to hide our struggle. **Bring those LIES in your mind to the light, and surrender them to God.** He will immerse you in His truth and show you that you are NOT damaged goods.

God's Word says that we are **"fearfully and wonderfully made"** in Psalm 139:14. God doesn't want us to be anxious.

Philippians 4:6-7 says,

"Do not be anxious about anything, but in every situation, by prayer and petition, with thanksgiving, present your requests to God. And the peace of God, which transcends all understanding, will guard your hearts and your minds in Christ Jesus."

And, Jesus tells us,
"Peace I leave with you; my peace I give you. I do not give to you as the world gives. Do not let your hearts be troubled and do not be afraid." John 14:27

Friend, anxiety and depression are not easy battles to face, and we certainly can't face them alone. If you are facing this, please open up to your spouse, trusted family member, or close friend. Find a local Christian counselor or pastor to talk to on a regular basis. Tell your doctor too. **In certain situations, anti-depressants or anti-anxiety medication may be helpful.**

You do not have to keep on suffering with this, and you *will* get through this.

There will come a day when you *will* walk in freedom. It may take some time–more time than you realize right now–but I promise you that freedom will come when you refuse to give up and continue to get the help that you need. **Let today be your first step to freedom, Friend.**

How to Use this Devotional

1. Read one verse and prayer per day.

Whether you complete it each morning or at night, try to do this devotional one day at a time. This will allow you to meditate on each verse and focus on one prayer for each day.

2.   Say the verses out loud.

This may seem silly or kind of weird, but it is actually Biblical. When Jesus was being tempted by Satan in the desert, He responded to him by saying scripture out loud. So, if Jesus did this, why not us? There is power in speaking God's Word out loud, and it also helps us to commit these Truths to memory.

3.   Don't rush it.

Find a cozy and quiet place where you can go each day to spend some time with God in prayer. Be sure to take your time when completing each day's devotion, and you will gain more peace and perspective. You may consider posting each day's verse in your car, on your fridge, at your desk, or on your bedside table to help fill your mind with these encouraging and uplifting Truths throughout the day.

4.   Write down your thoughts.

Journaling can be an extremely helpful way to process anxiety and depression. I highly encourage you to write down whatever is on your mind and in your heart after you read through the verses and say the prayer. You might even enjoy looking back at your journal entries at the end of the 31 days to see what God has done in your life.

A Note to Those Whose Spouse has Anxiety and/or Depression

We often use the terms "anxious" and "anxiety" to describe our nervousness or apprehension about something. But, for those who suffer with recurring anxiety attacks, we know all-to-well how real anxiety can interrupt our lives, steal our joy, and greatly affect our role as husbands or wives.

I have been suffering with anxiety since I was a young girl. What started as a little worry would quickly turn into a full-fledge crisis within my mind over time. There is a distinct difference between the non-anxious mind and the anxious mind...

Imagine that you are jumping off of a diving board into a swimming pool. As you plunge into the water, you start to sink down but quickly move your arms to make your way up to the surface to breathe.

This is how we are supposed to deal with worry. The worry may enter our minds, but we quickly find a way to find our way out of it...whether it be through talking about it, thinking about it, reading scripture, praying, etc.. When we handle worry normally, it is not a STAYING place. We just pass through it.

Now, imagine that you are jumping off the diving board, and the minute you hit the water you begin to sink lower and lower. Your arms don't move. Your chest feels the pressure from the lack of oxygen. You feel the enormous weight of the water all around you. You begin to move your arms back and forth, but you can't make your way up to the surface.

You are stuck. Paralyzed by fear. You want to make it up to the surface, but the weight is just too heavy.

This is exactly how it feels when we experience an anxiety attack or ongoing anxiety over time. It's more than a worrisome thought. We want to shake it off, but it's a much more complicated process for us.

Some of you know exactly what I am talking about, while others might see this kind of recurring struggle in their spouses. I am writing this note to you specifically with the hope that you will gain a greater understanding of what it really means to be anxious and how husbands and wives have a great capacity to help each other when one is facing anxiety.

Here are 5 things your anxious spouse wants you to know:

1. We are not crazy.
As I described earlier, an anxious mind certainly works differently than a non-anxious mind, but that doesn't mean that we are "crazy". Many times, an anxious person is hard to spot because we often put on a "happy face" and are highly-functioning. We try to hide our anxious episodes because we don't want to burden our families. But, we are not crazy. In fact, we are all-to-aware of our anxiety...and that causes us to spiral into more anxiety. The anxious person can have a hard time emotionally and mentally coping with life for a season or for many seasons.

2. We can often recognize our own anxiety for what it is.
Most of the time, we KNOW that we are not thinking clearly. We realize that we are anxious. We sincerely desire to get better, but we often don't know where to start. We feel like a sailboat just waiting for the wind to catch our sail. We can recognize that we NEED the wind, and we sincerely desire to get out of our anxious downhill spiral.

3. Our anxiety can be emotionally paralyzing and physically limiting at times.
I believe that this is the hardest one for those without anxiety to understand. When we experience anxious moments, our thoughts become stuck on the worry or stress that we are enduring. It's like a bird making a nest in our heads and then laying eggs. Then, the eggs hatch and, yes, more birds. Anxiety has a way of multiplying, and sometimes, it manifests itself into a full-blown anxiety attack. During an attack, our heart starts racing, we sweat, we can have stomach pains, nausea, vomiting, diarrhea, trouble breathing, and even heart palpitations. It paralyzes us for that moment and eventually passes, but it is as real as any sickness. And, therefore, we must get help.

4. We need your patience and compassion.
Overcoming anxiety is a process that often takes lots of prayer, time, and counseling. Sometimes, medication is needed to help our brains regain and maintain the proper levels of serotonin. I went through years of counseling before I felt like I was able to overcome my anxiety.

My husband, Dave, played an instrumental role in my recovery. He NEVER told me to "snap out of it". He would listen to me talk about my feelings for hours on end. He prayed with me constantly and would remind me of the truth of God's Word. He helped me to find a good counselor and showed me great compassion during the many nights I would cry myself to sleep.

I often felt guilty that I couldn't shake the anxiety, and I remember telling Dave that he deserved a better wife who wasn't crazy. He would always take my hands, stare straight into my eyes, and reassure me that I am his one and only and that we would get through this together. I don't think I would have recovered without his steadfast support, patience, and compassion. I am forever thankful to him for truly living out the marital vow of "in sickness and in health" during those long, difficult years.

5. Don't give up on us; there is HOPE in recovery.

I have experienced first hand that there is tremendous hope in recovery from anxiety. More than anything, we need to know that our spouse won't give up on us. Spouses, we need to know that you believe that we will get better. Please don't add to our anxiety by trying to rush our recovery process or doubting that we will ever be able to recover in the first place.

How You Can Use This Devotional to Help Your Spouse

1. Say these verses out loud to your spouse.

There is power in speaking verses out loud. Ask your spouse if you can share the verses with him/her, and if he/she agrees, say them aloud to him/her. You might even consider writing these verses down and posting them in places where your husband or wife can see them. You certainly don't want to bombard him/her with them, but little reminders of God's love and hope will be a great encouragement to him/her.

2. Replace the "I" or "Me" statements in the prayers with your husband's or wife's name.

Since you are doing this devotional to support your spouse's healing, it's important that you pray specifically for him/her. Whether you say these prayers in his or her presence or on your own, your prayers will be an important part of your spouse's healing process. And, God will use this prayer time to give you strength and perspective as well.

3. **Write down your thoughts.**

Trying to be supportive to a spouse with anxiety and/or depression can be very difficult. You are going to have feelings of anger, frustration, desperation, confusion, and even a little helplessness at times, and that is okay. It's hard. As you say these prayers, ask God to give you strength, grace, and patience as you try to support your spouse in this struggle. He will sustain you. Write down what you are feeling. This will help you to process everything. Then, after 31 days, go back and read what you wrote, and you will see how God has moved in your life and your spouse's life.

31 Verses and Prayers for the Anxious Mind and Heart
A Hope-filled and Healing Devotional for Those Who Struggle with Anxiety and Depression

Thoughts Before You Get Started...

DATE:_____

_____

_____

_____

_____

_____

_____

_____

_____

_____

_____

Day 1:

"Trust in the Lord with all your heart, and lean not on your own understanding. In all your ways acknowledge Him, and He will direct your path."
Proverbs 3:5-6

Dear Lord,
Bring peace to my wandering and worrisome thoughts today. Help me to remember that I don't have to "figure it out"; I just have to trust in You. Lord, thank You for being the constant in my life. Help me to trust in You—not my emotions, not another person, and not my own intellect. I trust You to carefully direct and keep my mind and heart today. Thank you, Lord.
In Jesus' Name,
Amen

How can you trust the Lord more today?

DATE:_____

_____

_____

_____

_____

_____

_____

_____

_____

_____

More Reflections

_____

_____

_____

_____

_____

_____

_____

_____

_____

_____

_____

_____

Day 2:

"The thief comes only to steal and kill and destroy; I have come that they may have life, and have it to the full."
John 10:10

Dear Lord,
Help me to realize that there is a spiritual battle after my mind and heart. There is a thief who wants to distract me, beat me down, and force me to give up. But, You are more powerful than anything the thief throws at me. Help me to remember that you sent your Son to die on the cross so that I can walk in freedom and live a full, vibrant, and focused life. Help me to stand strong in You today, Lord. And, help me to recognize these mental and emotional distractions for what they are—crafty thieves after my peace and joy. Take them down, Lord!
In Jesus' Name,
Amen

What lies are you believing as truths? What does the Word say about those lies?

DATE:_____

_____

_____

_____

_____

_____

_____

_____

_____

_____

More Reflections

_____

_____

_____

_____

_____

_____

_____

_____

_____

_____

_____

_____

Day 3:

"And the peace of God that surpasses all understanding will guard your hearts and minds in Christ Jesus…"
Philippians 4:7

Father,
My heart is heavy today. Sometimes, I feel like these condemning thoughts will never leave my mind. Remind me that I am not defined by these thoughts, and they have no power over me when I surrender them to You. Help me to feel your deep love for me, Lord. There is not one terrible thought or action that can separate me from Your love. Thank You, Lord! May Your peace—Your perfect peace—surround my mind and heart like a fortress against my anxieties.
In Jesus' Name,
Amen

What do you need to surrender to the Lord today?

DATE:_____

_____

_____

_____

_____

_____

_____

_____

_____

_____

More Reflections

_____

_____

_____

_____

_____

_____

_____

_____

_____

_____

_____

_____

Day 4:

"The Lord is close to the brokenhearted
and saves those who are crushed in
spirit."
Psalm 34:18

Dear Lord,
Thank You for your steadfast love.
Thank You for meeting me in the
midst of my pain and struggle.
Even when my spirit feels crushed,
You lift me up, dust me off, and
call me Chosen, Beloved, Child of
God. You mend my broken heart.
Help me to know and believe that
You are healing me little by little,
each and every day.
In Jesus' Name,
Amen

What breaks your heart?
Ask God to heal those areas of
hurt today.

DATE:_____

_____

_____

_____

_____

_____

_____

_____

_____

_____

_____

More Reflections

Day 5:

"Yes, my soul, find rest in God; my hope comes from him."
Psalm 62:5

Father,
I feel weak today. I'm exhausted from of night of worrying and toiling over thoughts. Sometimes, I'm even sickened by it all to the point that my stomach aches and churns. Lord, be my strength today. Take this restlessness from me. Bring peace to my mind, body, and soul. Thank You, Lord, for being my Hope. Help me to rest in You today.
In Jesus' Name,
Amen

How will you rest in the Lord today?

DATE:_____

_____

_____

_____

_____

_____

_____

_____

_____

_____

_____

More Reflections

_____

_____

_____

_____

_____

_____

_____

_____

_____

_____

_____

Day 6:

"No, in all these things we are more than conquerors through him who loved us. ..."
Romans 8:37

Dear Lord,
Help me to know that I won't have to live with anxiety and depression all of my life. Remind me that there is total victory in You. You are doing a work in me for my good and Your glory, and You waste nothing that I go through— the struggle and the healing. I am not a victim; I am a more than a conqueror in Christ. Give me strength to face each day. I am Yours, Lord.
In Jesus' Name,
Amen

What do you want the Lord to help you conquer today?

DATE:_____

_____

_____

_____

_____

_____

_____

_____

_____

_____

_____

More Reflections

Day 7:

"Finally, brothers and sisters, whatever is true, whatever is noble, whatever is right, whatever is pure, whatever is lovely, whatever is admirable—if anything is excellent or praiseworthy—think about such things."
Philippians 4:8

Heavenly Father,
Fill my mind with good thoughts. I praise Your name—even in the midst of my pain—because You love me and help me to walk in Your truth. Give me eyes that see goodness and beauty all around me. Give me ears that tune into beautiful melodies and affirming words. Give me a spirit of thankfulness and joy that cannot be poisoned by worry, fear, and negativity. Thank You for the work You are doing in me and through me, Lord. May You be glorified.
In Jesus' Name,
Amen

What are you thankful for today?

DATE:_____

_____

_____

_____

_____

_____

_____

_____

_____

_____

More Reflections

Day 8:

"Therefore, if anyone is in Christ, the new creation has come: The old has gone, the new is here!"
2 Corinthians 5:17

Dear Lord,
I'm feeling bogged down with regret today. I don't want my past failures to limit my future, and I sometimes run them like a movie reel through my mind. Lord, help me to know and believe that I have been made new in Christ. I am not held captive by my past. You forgive me of my sins every time I come to you with a repentant heart. I have been made new in Christ, and no part of my past can take that away from me. Thank You for the gift of salvation. Help me to fully accept this tremendous gift every day so that I may awake anew with a fresh mind and heart—ready to face each day with a clean slate.
In Jesus' Name,
Amen

How has God made you new? How can you embrace your "newness" more today?

DATE:_____

_____

_____

_____

_____

_____

_____

_____

_____

_____

More Reflections

Day 9:

"We demolish arguments and every pretension that sets itself up against the knowledge of God, and we take captive every thought to make it obedient to Christ."
2 Corinthians 10:5

Dear Lord,
I am weary today. I feel as if so many negative and condemning thoughts are riddling my mind like birds making a nest in my head. Lord, give me the strength of mind to command these nasty "birds" to fly away. They are not welcome. My mind is Yours and Yours alone. I want all of my thoughts to be filtered through Christ. If a thought is not based on Your truth, fitting with Your character, and glorifying to You, give me the strength and presence of mind to let it go. Help me to realize that I cannot always determine what thoughts pop into my mind, but I can choose what stays there. Thank You for filling my mind with Your Truth today.
In Jesus' Name,
Amen

What negative thoughts to you need to take captive today, and how can you replace those thoughts with the Truth?

DATE:_____

_____

_____

_____

_____

_____

_____

_____

_____

_____

_____

More Reflections

Day 10:

"Cast all your anxiety on him because he cares for you."
1 Peter 5:7

Father,
I realize that I can't face this anxiety alone. Sometimes, I feel like I am suffocating from the weight of it all. But, I know that You will not let this destroy me. I need Your strength to bear it. I give it over to You today. Take it all, Lord. Help me to feel the great weight lifted off of my mind and heart. Thank You for loving me so much so that You are willing to carry my burdens. How wonderful You are, Lord!
In Jesus' Name,
Amen

What are you anxious about today? Give them over to the Lord and trust that He will bring you peace.

DATE:_____

_____

_____

_____

_____

_____

_____

_____

_____

_____

_____

More Reflections

Day 11:

"Be strong and courageous. Do not be afraid or terrified because of them, for the Lord your God goes with you; he will never leave you nor forsake you."
Deuteronomy 31:6

Dear Lord,
I feel worn down today. Help me to know that my strength and courage come from You, and I must *choose* to be strong and courageous in You every day—even when I don't *feel* it. You help me to overcome my feelings when I trust in You and Your Truth. Help me to overcome my anxiety and depression today, Lord. I abide in You. Thank You in advance for what You are doing in me.
In Jesus' Name,
Amen

How can you be more courageous today?

DATE:_____

_____

_____

_____

_____

_____

_____

_____

_____

_____

_____

More Reflections

Day 12:

"'For I know the plans I have for you,' declares the Lord, 'plans to prosper you and not to harm you, plans to give you hope and a future.'"
Jeremiah 29:11

Dear Lord,
Sometimes I feel like I am damaged goods, and I will no longer be able to fulfill Your calling on my life because I am so down and out. I put on a happy face, but deep inside, I am fearful, anxious, and sad. Lord, remind me of Your wonderful plans for me. Help me to see that You made me for a distinct purpose, and You will use my bought with anxiety and depression for my good and Your glory. It is part of my story, but not all of my story. It will stand as a testimony of Your power, love, and grace. Tune my ears to Your voice of Truth, Lord. Give me a laser focus for all that You have for me.
In Jesus' Name,
Amen

What plans for your life has God placed in your heart? What steps can you take to pursue those plans?

DATE:_____

_____

_____

_____

_____

_____

_____

_____

_____

More Reflections

_____

_____

_____

_____

_____

_____

_____

_____

_____

_____

_____

_____

Day 13:

"There is no fear in love. But perfect love drives out fear, because fear has to do with punishment. The one who fears is not made perfect in love."
1 John 4:18

Father,
Thank You for loving me. I don't want to take your love for granted, but sometimes, I honestly fear that I do. I feel like I have let You down. But, Your Word tells me otherwise. Your Word—Your Truth— tells me that Your love dives to the depths of my pain. You are right here with me— holding me and comforting me. Thank You, Lord! Please cast out this fear inside my heart and replace it with Your perfect love.
In Jesus' Name,
Amen

What are your fears?
How can God's perfect Love and
Truth drive out those fears?

DATE:_____

_____

_____

_____

_____

_____

_____

_____

_____

_____

More Reflections

_____

_____

_____

_____

_____

_____

_____

_____

_____

_____

_____

_____

Day 14:

"But Jesus came and touched them. 'Get up,' he said. 'Don't be afraid.'"
Matthew 17:7

Dear Lord,
I don't feel like getting out of bed today. I'm tired and weary and frustrated with myself. Sometimes, I wonder why I keep trying. But, then I think about Jesus. I think about how He healed so many with just one touch —a powerful, life-changing touch that many couldn't fully understand. Help me to know and believe that You are healing me as well today. I receive Your healing touch today. Thank You, Lord! Help me to get up and face the day without fear and worry today.
In Jesus' Name,
Amen

What would you like Jesus to heal in you?

DATE:_____

_____

_____

_____

_____

_____

_____

_____

_____

_____

_____

More Reflections

_____

_____

_____

_____

_____

_____

_____

_____

_____

_____

_____

_____

Day 15:

"'I have told you these things, so that in me you may have peace. In this world you will have trouble. But take heart! I have overcome the world.'"
John 16:33

Heavenly Father,
I need Your peace today. I surrender all my worries, concerns, troubles, hangups, and frustrations to You. I realize that I am not being punished by all of this; troubles are part of being a human in this world. But, I am so thankful that You don't expect us to face our troubles alone. Calm my heart, Lord. Fill me with Your peace—Your perfect, lasting peace—today.
In Jesus' Name,
Amen

How can you experience more peace in the Lord today?

DATE:_____

_____

_____

_____

_____

_____

_____

_____

_____

_____

_____

More Reflections

_____

_____

_____

_____

_____

_____

_____

_____

_____

_____

_____

_____

Day 16:

"Consider it pure joy, my brothers and sisters, whenever you face trials of many kinds, because you know that the testing of your faith produces perseverance. Let perseverance finish its work so that you may be mature and complete, not lacking anything."
James 1:2-4

Dear Lord,
It's so hard not to allow these worrisome and condemning thoughts to hold me down. And, sometimes, I just want to give up and stay in bed all day. Give me the strength to persevere—to be there for my family, to get my work done, and do all the things You have called me to do. Help me to not see these people, places, and things as burdens, but as blessings. Increase my faith in You through these trials, Lord. I know You are helping me through this day by day. May I come through this struggle "mature and complete, not lacking anything."
In Jesus' Name,
Amen

In what areas of your life is God producing perseverance in you? Thank Him for this today.

DATE:_____

_____

_____

_____

_____

_____

_____

_____

_____

_____

More Reflections

Day 17:

"...seek peace and pursue it."
Psalm 34:14b

Father,
Help me to choose peace today.
Peace over production. Peace over
perception. Peace over perfection.
Settle my spirit, Lord. Give rest to
my weary heart. I know I can't live
the full life You want me to live
without peace, so I will consciously
pursue it with my mind and heart
every day. Give me peaceful
thoughts today, Lord. Thank You
for being my Prince of Peace.
In Jesus' Name,
Amen

What steps can you take to pursue peace today?

DATE:_____

_____

_____

_____

_____

_____

_____

_____

_____

_____

More Reflections

Day 18:

"...we know that suffering produces perseverance; perseverance, character; and character, hope. And hope does not put us to shame, because God's love has been poured out into our hearts through the Holy Spirit, who has been given to us."
Romans 5:3b-5

Dear Lord,
I know You are my healer, and I know You will heal me. But, I am so worn down in my suffering. My pain is not one that everyone can see, but I know You see it. And, I know You won't waste a single tear that I shed. Help me to see that there is purpose in this pain. I will have victory over my anxiety and depression, in Jesus' Name! Help me to persevere during this time. Your strength will help me to overcome my weakness. Grow my character and hope in You, Lord. I want my heart to overflow with Your love.
In Jesus' Name,
Amen

What are you hoping for today?

DATE:_____

_____

_____

_____

_____

_____

_____

_____

_____

_____

_____

More Reflections

Day 19:

"But I trust in your unfailing love; my heart rejoices in your salvation."
Psalm 13:5

Father,
Your love is amazing! Give me eyes to see and a heart to feel the tremendous love You have for me—even when I feel completely unlovable. Your love is sincere, unconditional, and life-changing—perfect. Nothing can separate me from Your love. You are carrying me through this struggle, Lord, and I thank You for that. Thank You for saving me. I wholly trust in You. All honor and glory and praise belongs to You!
In Jesus' Name,
Amen

How has God's love changed your life?

DATE:_____

_____

_____

_____

_____

_____

_____

_____

_____

_____

_____

More Reflections

Day 20:

"Therefore, as God's chosen people, holy and dearly loved, clothe yourselves with compassion, kindness, humility, gentleness and patience."
Colossians 3:12

Dear Lord,
Sometimes I look in the mirror, and I don't like what I see—physical and otherwise. I see a shadow of the person that I once was, and my heart aches for normalcy. Father, help me to see that You call me "chosen," "a masterpiece," and "a child of God." Help me to shed the labels that I or other people have tried to stick to me. Yours are the only ones that matter, because Yours are true. You are my Creator, my Father, my Friend, and my Savior. Thank You, Lord! May I put on your garments of love, compassion, kindness, humility, gentleness, and patience every day.
In Jesus' Name,
Amen

How can you show more compassion to your loved ones today?

DATE:_____

_____

_____

_____

_____

_____

_____

_____

_____

_____

More Reflections

Day 21:

"'Come to me, all you who are weary and burdened, and I will give you rest.'"
Matthew 11:28

Dear Lord,
Sometimes, I feel rejected and left out. I think my mind is playing tricks on me and skewing my judgment, but my jumbled thoughts and emotions make it unclear. Lord, help me to see Your truth in every situation. Thank You for always inviting me in and wanting to be with me. You don't shy away from me in this trial. You come to me with open arms, ready to comfort and bear the burden. What a great weight is lifted when I rest in You! Help me to fully surrender my anxieties to You today and experience the rest that You so freely give.
In Jesus' Name,
Amen

What is weighing you down today? Ask God to take these burdens and give you rest.

DATE:_____

_____

_____

_____

_____

_____

_____

_____

_____

_____

More Reflections

_____

_____

_____

_____

_____

_____

_____

_____

_____

_____

_____

Day 22:

"Therefore, there is now no condemnation for those who are in Christ Jesus."
Romans 8:1

Heavenly Father,
Thank You for this new day. I praise You for Your mercy and grace. Please take away my self-condemning thoughts, Lord. Help me to recognize them as the lies that they are. They are arrows shot by the accuser that is after my peace, but he cannot hurl anything at me that You cannot withstand and defeat. Build a fortress of strength around my mind and heart, Lord. You are my Lord and Savior, and You don't condemn me—You love me. Thank You, Lord! May Your love wash over me like a flood and fill every hole I have from insecurity, sadness, and shame.
In Jesus' Name,
Amen

What makes you feel insecure? How does God's love and strength help you to overcome these insecurities?

DATE:_____

_____

_____

_____

_____

_____

_____

_____

_____

_____

More Reflections

Day 23:

"And I pray that you, being rooted and established in love, may have power, together with all the Lord's holy people, to grasp how wide and long and high and deep is the love of Christ, and to know this love that surpasses knowledge—that you may be filled to the measure of all the fullness of God."
Ephesians 3:17b-19

Dear Lord,
I am on empty today. I so long to have my spark back, Lord. Reignite my passion for the gifts and talents that You have given me. Bring peace and focus to my mind, and help me to remain rooted in You and Your great love. I know I will never be able to fully understand Your love, but I receive it as the amazing, far-reaching, mind-boggling gift that it is. May I love my family, my friends, my neighbors, my co-workers, and myself more because of Your unending love.
In Jesus' Name,
Amen

What steps can you take to be more rooted in God's love today?

DATE:_____

_____

_____

_____

_____

_____

_____

_____

_____

_____

More Reflections

Day 24:

"For God did not give us a spirit of fear, but of power and love and of a sound mind."
2 Timothy 1:7 (NHEB)

Father,
This struggle with anxiety and depression makes me feel like there is chaos all around me. But, Your Word says that You are a God of order. You carefully crafted my mind and heart with a special purpose in Your mind, and You created me to be in line with Your character and ways. Bring peace to my mind and heart today, Lord. Help me to feel Your calming Spirit like a refreshing breeze over my anxious soul.
In Jesus' Name,
Amen

How can you experience calmness in the Lord today?

DATE:_____

_____

_____

_____

_____

_____

_____

_____

_____

_____

_____

More Reflections

Day 25:

"Shout for joy, you heavens; rejoice, you earth; burst into song, you mountains! For the Lord comforts his people and will have compassion on his afflicted ones."
Isaiah 49:13

Dear Lord,
Sometimes, I just wish I could snap out of this funk, but I can't. I need Your power to help me overcome this battle. I get so frustrated with myself when I try to find freedom from this on my own. But, when I come to You with my burdens, You have compassion for me. You are not a distant Father. You draw me close with Your loving arms and lean over to whisper, "It's going to be okay. I am with you." Thank You for loving me enough to meet me here— even on my lowest days. I sing Your praises, Lord, even though I am in the midst of this struggle. I will praise You through it all because I know that You are with me. I love You, Lord!
In Jesus' Name,
Amen

In what ways are you feeling God's comfort and compassion for you today?

DATE:_____

_____

_____

_____

_____

_____

_____

_____

_____

_____

More Reflections

Day 26:

"When you pass through the waters,
  I will be with you;
and when you pass through the rivers,
  they will not sweep over you.
When you walk through the fire,
  you will not be burned;
  the flames will not set you ablaze."
Isaiah 43:2

Heavenly Father,
There are days when I honestly feel like I
am drowning. The weight of these anxieties
are so heavy on my mind and heart. But,
You promise that You will never give me
more than I can bear with Your strength.
Help me to know and believe this today. Let
this truth ring through my ears and resonate
in my heart. Thank You for never leaving
me, Father. Be my strength and stay today.
In Jesus' Name,
Amen

What is overwhelming you to-day? Ask God to rescue you from this, and believe that He will do it.

DATE:_____

_____

_____

_____

_____

_____

_____

_____

_____

_____

More Reflections

Day 27:

"For I am convinced that neither death nor life, neither angels nor demons, neither the present nor the future, nor any powers, neither height nor depth, nor anything else in all creation, will be able to us from the love of God that is in Christ Jesus our Lord."
Romans 8:38-39

Dear Lord,
I find such comfort in knowing that nothing can separate me from you—no worry, no anxiety, no sadness, no past decisions, no present crisis, and no future problem. You are with me always. Thank You, Lord! Help me to feel Your presence today. May I approach this day as one who knows that I am fiercely and completely loved by You—my God, my Creator, my Sustainer, my Savior, and my Healer.
In Jesus' Name,
Amen

What do you need to let go from your past? Confess these things to the Lord, and trust that He is setting you free today.

DATE:_____

_____

_____

_____

_____

_____

_____

_____

_____

_____

More Reflections

Day 28:

"No temptation has overtaken you except what is common to mankind. And God is faithful; he will not let you be tempted beyond what you can bear. But when you are tempted, he will also provide a way out so that you can endure it."
1 Corinthians 10:13

Dear Lord,
Guide my mind to think on things that are of You today. Protect my heart from the weariness that wants to seep in. Keep my doubts at bay, Lord, and replace those doubts with the assurance of Your love for me. When I am tempted to give myself over to worries, sadness, and lies, help me to stand strong and to see a way out of it. You are in control, Lord. I fully surrender my mind and heart to You.
In Jesus' Name,
Amen

What temptations are you experiencing today? Ask God to give you a way to overcome them in His strength.

DATE:_____

_____

_____

_____

_____

_____

_____

_____

_____

_____

More Reflections

Day 29:

"And the God of all grace, who called you to his eternal glory in Christ, after you have suffered a little while, will himself restore you and make you strong, firm and steadfast."
1 Peter 5:10

Father,
Thank You for Your grace and mercy. It baffles me to think that You sent Your Son, Jesus, to die for me and my sins. Thank You! Jesus told us that we would not be immune to troubles, but sometimes, my anxiety and depression seem like too heavy a burden to bear. Lord, please show me the promise of a life lived without this burden. Give me little glimpses of hope and freedom today. I cling to the Your promises! I know You always fulfill them. I am believing that You are making me strong, firm, and steadfast through this trial. And, I know my day of full restoration is coming, but I desperately need You to sustain me while I wait.
In Jesus' Name,
Amen

What would you like God to restore in your life?

DATE:_____

_____

_____

_____

_____

_____

_____

_____

_____

_____

More Reflections

Day 30:

"But he said to me, 'My grace is sufficient for you, for my power is made perfect in weakness.' Therefore I will boast all the more gladly about my weaknesses, so that Christ's power may rest on me."
2 Corinthians 12:9

Dear Lord,
I believe You are going to use my trial with anxiety and depression and turn it into an amazing testimony to help others dealing with the same things. This brings me great joy! I know You always have a plan, and You never waste any of our pain. Give me strength to share my struggle with others so that You may be glorified in my weakness.
In Jesus' Name,
Amen

What makes you feel weak? How is God showing His strength in your weakness?

DATE:_____

_____

_____

_____

_____

_____

_____

_____

_____

_____

More Reflections

Day 31:

"...but those who hope in the Lord will renew their strength. They will soar on wings like eagles; they will run and not grow weary, they will walk and not be faint."
Isaiah 40:31

Father,
You are my hope. You are my strength.
You are my Healer. Thank You, Lord!
Help me to see that You are making me
stronger through this struggle. Little
my little, You are renewing my
strength. I so long for the day that I
will soar and be free from this burden.
But, until then, I will praise You and
believe that freedom is coming. I thank
You in advance of what You are doing
in me and through me, Lord. To You
be all honor, glory, and praise forever!
In Jesus' Name,
Amen

How has God renewed your hope through the last 31 days? Thank Him for all He has done and will continue to do in you and through you.

DATE:_____

_____

_____

_____

_____

_____

_____

_____

_____

_____

More Reflections

_____

_____

_____

_____

_____

_____

_____

_____

_____

_____

_____

_____

Next Steps

Congratulations! You have completed 31 days of prayer to help you overcome your anxiety and/or depression. You have also read 31 essential verses and hopefully committed many of them to memory. Way to go! It is my hope and prayer that you felt a great weight lifted with each verse that you read and prayer that you prayed. More than anything, I hope you grew in your relationship with the Lord and know, with all of your heart and all of your mind, that He is Your Healer.

So, what now?

Here are some practical next steps to consider:

1. Go through the 31 days of verses and prayers AGAIN.

Hey, who ever said you can only do this for one month? These verses and prayers are powerful, and the more you speak them out loud, the more they will fill your mind and heart and focus your mind on the Lord. So, if you'd like to go through it again, then go for it!

2. Find a local Christian counselor.

As I stated at the beginning of the devotional, I am a HUGE proponent of Christian counseling. In fact, it was a big part of my own recovery. If you'd like to talk to a Christian counselor, you can find one near you by going to http://www.aac-c.net/resources/find-a-counselor/ . You might also consider asking your pastor at your church for some counselor recommendations.

3. Find a local support group.

It helps to know that we are not alone in our struggles. That is precisely why support groups are so helpful. If you'd like to meet with others who are going through or have been through anxiety and depression, you might consider joining a local support group. You can find one near you by going to http://www.celebraterecovery.com or by calling your church office and asking for recommendations.

Whatever next steps you decide to do, keep on reading the Word, committing verses to memory, praying for your recovery, and talking to your spouse and other trusted loved ones about your struggle.

God is with you and for you, sweet friend. May you walk in the freedom and splendor of His love and strength. Be blessed!

For more resources, go to DaveAndAshleyWillis.com.

About the Author:

Ashley Willis is a wife, mommy of four little boys, speaker, writer and entrepreneur. She's a popular blogger on topics related to marriage, faith, family, motherhood, and her own struggle with anxiety and depression. Ashley has a passion for encouraging and inspiring others through her books, blogs, videos and speaking events, but her favorite thing to do is to travel to new and exciting places with her "five guys". If you'd like to connect with Ashley and check out her other resources, go to www.DaveAndAshleyWillis.com.

12621582R20085

Made in the USA
Monee, IL
27 September 2019